The New Novello Choral Edition

JOSEPH HAYDN

'Maria Theresa' Mass
Theresienmesse

(Hob. XXII: 12)

for soprano, alto, tenor and bass soli, SATB choir and orchestra

Vocal score

Revised by Michael Pilkington

Order No: NOV078474

NOVELLO PUBLISHING LIMITED

PREFACE

Haydn composed the *Maria Theresa Mass* in 1799, between the *Creation* and the *Seasons*. The first performance took place on the name-day of the princess Maria Josepha Hermangild, wife of Haydn's employer prince Nikolas Esterházy, for whom he had already written four masses for similar occasions. It was performed in the court chapel in Vienna as early as May 1800, and probably earned its name 'Theresa Mass' soon after, in reference to the Empress Maria Theresa of Austria. This edition is based on that presented in Joseph Haydn Werke Series XXIII vol. 3, edited by Günter Thomas, with a new piano reduction by the present editor. The following sources were used by Günter Thomas:

A The autograph score, Austrian National Library, Vienna.

B A set of parts, mostly copied by Haydn's personal copyist Johann Elssler; Esterházy Archives, Eisenstadt.

C A set of parts, copied by Ellsler, National Museum, Prague; this follows the Eisenstadt parts.

D A set of parts, Hofmusikkapelle, Vienna.

Thomas frequently refers to the 'authentic copies' presumably meaning sources **B** - **D**; though he does not distinguish between them.

All additions or modifications of the original score are indicated by square brackets, strokes through slurs and hairpins, or footnotes.

Kyrie: in bar 102 the soprano grace note should come on the beat. There should be a diminuendo for all voices through b.103, though it may well be that Haydn intended a *subito p* at b.104.

Gloria, bb.81 and 83: the old Novello edition has d' and b flat as the first notes in these bars for tenor and bass; Thomas gives c' and a without comment, but the Novello emendation seems reasonable in the light of the unchanging orchestral harmony.

Agnus Dei bb.169-70: thomas gives parts for strings 'after authentic copies', but why add them here and not in bb.152-3?

A few problems arise in the parts for the soloists. Ambiguity arises from the eighteenth century system of using the same staves for both soloists and chorus. In bar 321 of the Gloria, the entry of the soloists is ignored in the old Novello vocal score, similarly in bar 335. Bars 320 and 334 have 'tutti' on the vocal staves, though the parts for soloist and chorus are clearly different in this bar. Thomas makes no comment in adding the soloists in bars 321 and 335; other editors give double stems for these bars, though not continuing with them to the end of the phrase. In bars 49 and 50 of the Benedictus, Thomas gives the Alto part double stems, for the soloist to join the chorus altos, but does not continue with them over the page. At bar 110 double stems are only given for the first two notes. At bars 133-5 the soprano soloist is only given 'in excelsis' once. In all these instances, the soloists should surely continue to the end of the phrase. In most early performances, the soloists would, in any case, have been members of the choir and have sung throughout.

Michael Pilkington
Old Coulsdon
May 2001

Cover illustration:portrait of the Empress Maria Theresa of Austria (1717-1780) by Martin Meytens (1695-1770) and studio. Courtesy of the Kunsthistorisches Museum, Vienna (Bridgeman Art Library).

© 2001 Novello & Company Limited
Published in Great Britain by Novello Publishing Limited - Head Office: 14-15 Berners Street, London W1T 3LJ
Tel +44 (0)20 7612 7400   Fax +44 (0)20 7612 7546
Sales and Hire: Music Sales Distribution Centre - Newmarket Road, Bury St Edmunds, Suffolk IP33 3YB
Tel +44 (0)1284 702600   Fax +44 (0)1284 768301
Web: www.chesternovello.com   e-mail: music@musicsales.co.uk
All rights reserved   Printed in Great Britain
Music setting by Stave Origination

MARIA THERESA MASS
Theresienmesse

JOSEPH HAYDN

KYRIE

* All voices beat 3: ♪ 𝄾 , Thomas, 'after the authentic copies', noting that autograph reads ♩, all voices   † see Preface

GLORIA
GLORIA IN EXCELSIS

* see Preface

GRATIAS

23

QUONIAM

* Alto: f' in sources, but see violin 2 and octaves with tenor

CREDO
CREDO IN UNUM DEUM

* RH bar 21 notes 1-5: f"c"f"f"f"; bar 24 note 13 and bar 25 note 5: d"; Thomas, 'after the authentic copies', see Preface

ET INCARNATUS EST

ET RESURREXIT

* Bass notes 2-3: g f♯ in sources, but see orchestral bass

* Bass beat 1: rhythm ♩ ♪ in sources

SANCTUS

BENEDICTUS

* Bass notes 5-6 ♯ in sources

* see Preface

* RH note 10: Thomas suggests d''' for c''', given in all sources

AGNUS DEI

DONA NOBIS PACEM

* 'dolce' added to autograph in pencil

* Bass note 1: d in sources, but see orchestral bass and bar 93

* Bars 169-70: orchestral parts 'after the authentic copies', Thomas, see Preface

Printed and bound in Great Britain by Caligraving Limited

8 9 10 11 12 13 14 15 16 17 18 19 20